Greetings!

We can't even express how excited we are that you're taking this journey with us toward debt-free living. As you've been reading in our book, our actions early on in our marriage set us up for years of pain and turmoil in the area of our finances, which ultimately spilled into the rest of our lives. Our hope for you is that no matter where you are on your journey, you use our book—and these worksheets—to help you.

These worksheets coordinate with the content provided in our book, The 2% Rule To Get Debt Free Fast. We encourage you to read our book to gain the context you need to fill out each worksheet. You will see short instructions are included at the top of each worksheet with a reference to our book to so you can get additional information.

You will also see we have divided the worksheets into five separate sections to help guide you in your journey.

Part I will provide you the worksheets as you prepare to start your journey. One wise man once said, "Every journey begins with a single step." Your financial journey's first step involves you and your family getting on the same page about your finances and goals. We encourage you to start here as this will prepare you for the remaining steps.

Part II will provide you the spreadsheets for the full implementation of our 2% Rule. Obviously you will need to reference the book to learn more about this approach, but these sheets should help you each step of the way.

Part III provides worksheets to assist you in that seemingly overwhelming step of finding ways to bring in extra income. As you work through these worksheets, allow them to help you take baby steps and find the path that works best for you.

Part IV lists worksheets that will help you find that 2% cut each and every month. Many of these tools will give you exactly what you need to keep shrinking that budget one step at a time.

Finally, Part V will give you some worksheets to help you take those next steps in your process.

Know we are cheering you on as you work through this plan and make it fit to your family. Take a deep breath, set your mindset toward being intentional, and let's get started!

Take care,

Alex and Cassie Michael

Checklist for Debt-Free Living

Done	Completion Date	Step
☐		Step 1—Build Emergency Fund Quickly
☐		Step 2—Pay Off All Consumer Debt Using 2% Rule
☐		Step 3—Set-up Bi-Weekly Mortgage Payments
☐		Step 4—Contribute The Maximum on your 401(k) for Company Match
☐		Step 5—Build 3 to 6 Months of Savings
☐		Step 6—Contribute The Remaining Retirement 15% into a Roth IRA
☐		Step 7—Set up your Cash and Percentage Based Savings Amounts and Add Your Contributions
☐		Step 8—Contribute the Maximum Household Allowance for a Roth IRA
☐		Step 9—Round Mortgage Payments to the Nearest $100
☐		Step 10—Fund Businesses
☐		Step 11—Pay Extra Towards Mortgage
☐		Step 12—Implement the 7-10 Mortgage Plan
☐		Step 13—Decide Your Next Financial Investments and Steps

Part I

GETTING STARTED

Be Intentional Questionnaire

The intent of this questionnaire is to identify your obstacles and barriers in daily life. It is simply to identify and become aware so that you can "reset" your mindset to one of becoming more intentional in all that you say and want to do. Refer to Chapters 1 and 20 for additional information.

This worksheet can and should be filled out by each participating family member and then as the family as a whole.

Identify Your Obstacles

1. Thinking about your daily life, what are obstacles that keep you from staying on track?

_____

_____

_____

2. Do you wake up and go to bed at the times you intend? What is working? What obstacles keep you from accomplishing this and what can you do to rectify it?

_____

_____

_____

3. Do you make the meals you intend to make each day?

_____

_____

_____

3a. If not, what are the obstacles preventing you from preparing meals?

_____

_____

_____

3b. If so, what aspect of this is working?

_____

_____

_____

4. Do you spend more money daily than you intend to?

_____

_____

_____

4a. What are the primary causes of this? Lack of prep? Laziness? Never really intentionally thought about it? Etc.

_____

_____

_____

5. If you have set a budget, have you been able to stick to it?

_____

_____

_____

5a. What is preventing you from sticking with it?

_____

_____

_____

6. Identify the top three major obstacles in your daily life that prevent you from accomplishing these daily tasks and goals?

_____

_____

_____

6a. Can you do something about these obstacles?

_____

_____

_____

6b. If yes, what?

_____

_____

_____

6c. If no, what is a work around?

_____

_____

_____

Annual Financial Summary

Schedule some time with your family to go through this questionnaire altogether.

Overall Goals

What overall goals do we have for our family?
This can include non-financial goals as well, as every decision truly has a financial impact on the family. Unless the goals are identified and prepared for in advance, those last-minute preparations could be costly. Alternatively, if you don't financially plan for those large dreams of the family, they may never come to fruition.

Long term (3+ years):

Mid term (1–3 years):

Short term (this year):

Specific Goals For This Year

What savings goals do we want to achieve?

Are we trying to pay off debt? How much? Do we have a plan of attack?

What charities do we wish to support this year:

Do we want to plan on a vacation(s) this year? How much should we budget?
The goal here isn't to plan the details, but to keep the questions at a high level (the 30,000-foot view). Do you want to drive or fly? Is this a 2-week vacation or a couple of weekend camping trips?

How much should we budget for Christmas?
Start thinking now about what we would like to set aside for Christmas. Can we develop a plan to set aside a certain amount per month to get to our goal?

What events are coming up this year?
Birthdays, anniversary, celebration?

Do we need to prepare for a major purchase this year?

Plan Of Action
What are some initial actions we need to implement to meet the identified goals? In the following weeks we will be identifying a more detailed approach – allow this meeting time to be a brainstorming session. Can you eliminate one or more meal out each month? Spend less on entertainment? Other ideas?
Do we want to work extra as a family to help with our goals? What are the talents of each family member? Is someone good with marketing? With numbers?
What expectations do we have of each family member?
What is one thing each family member is willing to sacrifice to meet our goals?
Can we as a family commit to reaching the goals we've decided upon?
How are we going to keep each other accountable?

Expense Tracking to Create Starter Budget

Track your spending in the following categories for one month. These do not include monthly payments on debt. This just your monthly living expenses and ongoing bills (like utilities). Use the blank lines to add any additional categories specific to you and your family. See additional details and full explanation in Chapter 2.

Living Expenses
- Groceries
- Gasoline
- Clothing
- Entertainment
- Eating Out
- Home Improvement
- Christmas and other Holidays
- Travel
- Miscellaneous Shopping (e.g. crafts, school supplies)

Bills
- Auto Expenses
- Insurance
- Utilities
- Cell Phones
- Internet
- Cable/Television services
- Services/fees

Other:

_____

_____

_____

This is your budget. From this point, the goal is to spend 2% less each month until you hit your rock bottom budget.

Why Do You Want To Be Debt Free or Financially Stable?

Directions to both spouses: In this worksheet, we want you to think about what motivates you and the reasons why you picked up this book and workbook and why you want to become debt free or in a better place financially? It could be for something like peace of mind, it could be for you and your children's future, it could even be something like "travel the world." Opening the lines of communication with your spouse is of super importance to this process. This worksheet is designed for each of you to fill out and discuss. See Chapters 5 & 19.

Define your reasons for debt freedom and/or financial stability

1. Take time to brainstorm all the reasons you want your family to be debt free and/or financially stable.

_____

_____

_____

2. What are you top three reasons?

_____

_____

_____

3. Which is your top reason?

_____

_____

_____

4. Compare these with lists from your spouse. Which reasons line up? Which reasons don't?

_____

_____

_____

5. Is there a way your top reason and your spouse's top reasons could be combined to give you a common vision?

_____

_____

_____

5a, If so then what is your combined vision?

_____

_____

_____

5b. If not then how can you work together to find a common vision to work together?

_____

_____

_____

Define the Path to Your Family's Success

This is a family roadmap to keep your family accountable. Fill this out altogether so you can agree on how to approach your debt payoff plan. Reference Chapter 19 for more information.

Intentionally Establish Your Plans

Establish meeting dates/times:

1. Daily check-in:

_____

_____

_____

1a. Meeting(s) to pay bills each week/month:

_____

_____

_____

1b. Meeting(s) to review last/next month's budgets:

_____

_____

_____

2. Monthly spending threshold:

_____

_____

_____

3. Allowance for kids:

_____

_____

_____

4. Breakdown of budgeting roles/tasks:

_____

_____

_____

Financial Questionnaire

Each spouse should fill out this questionnaire separately then come together to discuss the answers. Realize this is an opportunity to share your values while at the same time hearing the values of your spouse. Use this as a time to understand each other more and learn how to walk together united while considering each other's desires. See Chapter 5 for additional information.

What are your top five financial and purchasing priorities?

1. _____
2. _____
3. _____
4. _____
5. _____

If money were no object, what are your top dream goals and wants?

_____
_____
_____

How important are your wants?

_____
_____
_____

What do healthy finances look like to you?

_____
_____
_____

What are the things you value the most?

_____
_____
_____

How do you feel about debt?

_____

_____

_____

Do you want to be debt free? Why or why not?

_____

_____

_____

What are your goals for the next year?

_____

_____

_____

What are your goals for the next five years?

_____

_____

_____

What are your long-term goals?

_____

_____

_____

Do you have any other financial or life goals?

_____

_____

_____

What are your retirement goals (age to retire, desired lifestyle)?

_____

_____

_____

Identifying Spending Weaknesses

Each member of the family that has the ability to spend money should fill out this worksheet. Nearly all of us will have a "spending" or "money" weakness. It is important to identify your spending weaknesses, along with the weaknesses of your spouse and older children. See Chapter 6 for more details and for what our weaknesses were.

1. In everyday life, what items, events, or temptations do you tend to spend the most money on or are most tempted by?

_____

_____

_____

2. How often do you give into your spending temptation?

_____

_____

_____

3. What factors make it more difficult to resist (e.g. sale/coupon, shopping with friends, shopping online, when feeling down, etc.)

_____

_____

_____

4. In what, scalable, real ways can you avert these temptations?

_____

_____

_____

5. What do you need from your spouse/older children to help you avoid these temptations?

_____

_____

_____

Mindset Questionnaire
Reference chapter 9 for more information.

Determine

1. What have been the major influences in your life?

_____

_____

_____

1a. Who have been the major influencers in your life?

_____

_____

_____

1b. What are your life experiences?

_____

_____

_____

1c. What trials have you experienced?

_____

_____

_____

1d. What cultural influences have you experienced?

_____

_____

_____

1e. What influences do peer groups and other people exert?

_____

_____

_____

1f. What are your family influences?

_____

_____

_____

1g. What are your religious influences?

_____

_____

_____

Define
2. Define what you want your mindset to be.

_____

_____

_____

Decide
3. Make that intentional decision about what you want your mindset to tell you

_____

_____

_____

Shape
4. Write out your *Financial Vision Statement?*

_____

_____

_____

4a. Set your goals (long term, short term, big and small goals):

_____

_____

_____

Drive
5. Establish how you will remind yourself daily of your new mindset, vision, and goals.

_____

_____

Emergency Fund Worksheet

Determine how much of an emergency fund you need and then brainstorm with your family on the best way to build it. Reference Chapters 10 & 15 for more information.

1. How much of an emergency fund do I need?

_____

_____

_____

2. Determine whether you should save 1-2% of your gross annual income:

    Answer the following questions:

Yes	No	
☐	☐	Do you have any major appliances greater than 10 years old?
☐	☐	Do you have a vehicle with more than 100,000 miles?
☐	☐	Do you have more than four people in your household?
☐	☐	Do you have a home insurance deductible greater than or equal to $1000?
☐	☐	Is your home over 20 years old?
☐	☐	Over the past year have you had more than one emergency expense?
☐	☐	Do you have aging pets?

If you answered Yes to two or more of these questions, we recommend you consider an emergency fund of 2% of your annual income. Obviously this will depend on income as well as any other considerations you might have for your specific family.

Your Emergency Fund Percent: _____ %

3. Calculate the amount of emergency fund you need to set aside:

Total Gross Annual Household Income _____
Emergency Fund Percent: X _____ %
Your Emergency Fund = _____

Build your emergency fund quickly

Brainstorm ways as a family you can quickly save the total amount for your emergency fund. We have listed some ideas below to help get you started. For the ideas you choose to use, estimate the amount you hope to obtain from that effort and how much time it will take to save it in total. Refer to Chapter 15 for initial ideas and amounts.

Ideas to get started	Estimated Savings Amount

Be Intentional

As your emergency fund is not your FUN-d, how do you plan to keep this separate from your monthly budget?

Part II

THE 2% RULE

Debt payoff plans and goals

Reference Chapter 8 for completed examples and additional details on how to fill out this worksheet. This worksheet will help you identify your total amount of debts and prepare you for the next step in the debt payoff.

Full Debt Overview—Tip: Record all of your debts, including credit cards, credit lines, automobiles, student loans, etc. This is the fact-collecting process to help you open your eyes to your total debt load.						
Debt	Monthly Payment	Interest Rate	Lifetime Interest	Balance	Minimum Payment Payoff Time	Fixed or Adjustable Payment

Debt payoff plan

Follow the steps detailed in Chapter 8 to organize and prioritize your debt payoff strategy. After you finish this worksheet you will have a clear picture forward on your plan to pay off your debt.

Overview of Debt Payoff Plan—*Tip: Determine priority in each group based on balance, interest rate and payment amount. The more cash you can find available in a short amount of time, the faster the overall payoff.*

Debt	Interest Rate	Balance	Priority	Goal Payoff Date	Monthly Payment
$0–$1,500					
___	___	___	___	___	___
___	___	___	___	___	___
___	___	___	___	___	___
$1,501–$5,000					
___	___	___	___	___	___
___	___	___	___	___	___
___	___	___	___	___	___
$5,001–$10,000					
___	___	___	___	___	___
___	___	___	___	___	___
___	___	___	___	___	___
>$10,000					
___	___	___	___	___	___
___	___	___	___	___	___
___	___	___	___	___	___

Monthly Budget Planners

Use the following budget planners to set and track each month's budget and goals

Month 1

MON	TUE	WED	THU	FRI	SAT	SUN

Month at a Glance	
	Month
Starting Balance	

Bills	
Home	$_____
Auto	$_____
Auto Insurance	$_____
Gasoline	$_____
Groceries	$_____
Electric	$_____
Gas	$_____
Water	$_____
Cell Phone	$_____
Allowance	$_____

Income	
_____.	$_____
_____.	$_____
_____.	$_____
Total: $_____	

Savings	
Starting Balance	$_____
Deposit	$_____
Deposit	$_____
Deposit	$_____
Ending Balance	$_____

Monthly Budgeted Amount	
Entertainment	$_____
Clothing	$_____
Home	$_____
Eating Out	$_____
Travel	$_____
Medical	$_____
Auto	$_____
Christmas	$_____
	$_____
	$_____
	$_____
Ending Balance $_____	

Monthly Goals	
Projected	**Actual**
2% Increase	
2% Decrease	
Debt Paid Off	
Debts Paid Toward	
Total Amount Paid	

Month 2

MON	TUE	WED	THU	FRI	SAT	SUN

Month at a Glance	
Starting Balance	Month

Bills	
Home	$_____
Auto	$_____
Auto Insurance	$_____
Gasoline	$_____
Groceries	$_____
Electric	$_____
Gas	$_____
Water	$_____
Cell Phone	$_____
Allowance	$_____

Income	
_____ .	$ _____
_____ .	$ _____
_____ .	$ _____
Total: $ _____	

Savings	
Starting Balance	$ _____
Deposit	$ _____
Deposit	$ _____
Deposit	$ _____
Ending Balance	$ _____

Monthly Budgeted Amount	
Entertainment	$ _____
Clothing	$ _____
Home	$ _____
Eating Out	$ _____
Travel	$ _____
Medical	$ _____
Auto	$ _____
Christmas	$ _____
	$ _____
	$ _____
	$ _____
Ending Balance $ _____	

Monthly Goals	
Projected	**Actual**
2% Increase	
2% Decrease	
Debt Paid Off	
Debts Paid Toward	
Total Amount Paid	

Month 3

MON	TUE	WED	THU	FRI	SAT	SUN

Month at a Glance	
Starting Balance	Month

Bills	
Home	$_____
Auto	$_____
Auto Insurance	$_____
Gasoline	$_____
Groceries	$_____
Electric	$_____
Gas	$_____
Water	$_____
Cell Phone	$_____
Allowance	$_____

Income

_____.	$_____
_____.	$_____
_____.	$_____
Total: $_____	

Savings

Starting Balance	$_____
Deposit	$_____
Deposit	$_____
Deposit	$_____
Ending Balance	$_____

Monthly Budgeted Amount

Entertainment	$_____
Clothing	$_____
Home	$_____
Eating Out	$_____
Travel	$_____
Medical	$_____
Auto	$_____
Christmas	$_____
	$_____
	$_____
	$_____

Ending Balance $_____

Monthly Goals

Projected	Actual
2% Increase	
2% Decrease	
Debt Paid Off	
Debts Paid Toward	
Total Amount Paid	

Month 4

MON	TUE	WED	THU	FRI	SAT	SUN

Month at a Glance	
Starting Balance	Month

Bills	
Home	$_____
Auto	$_____
Auto Insurance	$_____
Gasoline	$_____
Groceries	$_____
Electric	$_____
Gas	$_____
Water	$_____
Cell Phone	$_____
Allowance	$_____

Income	
_____.	$_____
_____.	$_____
_____.	$_____
Total: $_____	

Savings	
Starting Balance	$_____
Deposit	$_____
Deposit	$_____
Deposit	$_____
Ending Balance	$_____

Monthly Budgeted Amount	
Entertainment	$_____
Clothing	$_____
Home	$_____
Eating Out	$_____
Travel	$_____
Medical	$_____
Auto	$_____
Christmas	$_____
	$_____
	$_____
	$_____
Ending Balance $_____	

Monthly Goals	
Projected	**Actual**
2% Increase	
2% Decrease	
Debt Paid Off	
Debts Paid Toward	
Total Amount Paid	

Month 5

MON	TUE	WED	THU	FRI	SAT	SUN

Month at a Glance	
Starting Balance	Month

Bills	
Home	$_____
Auto	$_____
Auto Insurance	$_____
Gasoline	$_____
Groceries	$_____
Electric	$_____
Gas	$_____
Water	$_____
Cell Phone	$_____
Allowance	$_____

Income	
_____.	$_____
_____.	$_____
_____.	$_____
Total: $_____	

Savings	
Starting Balance	$_____
Deposit	$_____
Deposit	$_____
Deposit	$_____
Ending Balance	$_____

Monthly Budgeted Amount	
Entertainment	$_____
Clothing	$_____
Home	$_____
Eating Out	$_____
Travel	$_____
Medical	$_____
Auto	$_____
Christmas	$_____
	$_____
	$_____
	$_____
Ending Balance $_____	

Monthly Goals	
Projected	**Actual**
2% Increase	
2% Decrease	
Debt Paid Off	
Debts Paid Toward	
Total Amount Paid	

Month 6

MON	TUE	WED	THU	FRI	SAT	SUN

Month at a Glance	
Starting Balance	Month

Bills	
Home	$_____
Auto	$_____
Auto Insurance	$_____
Gasoline	$_____
Groceries	$_____
Electric	$_____
Gas	$_____
Water	$_____
Cell Phone	$_____
Allowance	$_____

Income	
_____.	$_____
_____.	$_____
_____.	$_____
Total: $_____	

Savings	
Starting Balance	$_____
Deposit	$_____
Deposit	$_____
Deposit	$_____
Ending Balance	$_____

Monthly Budgeted Amount	
Entertainment	$_____
Clothing	$_____
Home	$_____
Eating Out	$_____
Travel	$_____
Medical	$_____
Auto	$_____
Christmas	$_____
	$_____
	$_____
	$_____
Ending Balance $_____	

Monthly Goals	
Projected	**Actual**
2% Increase	
2% Decrease	
Debt Paid Off	
Debts Paid Toward	
Total Amount Paid	

Month 7

MON	TUE	WED	THU	FRI	SAT	SUN

Month at a Glance	
Starting Balance	Month

Bills	
Home	$_____
Auto	$_____
Auto Insurance	$_____
Gasoline	$_____
Groceries	$_____
Electric	$_____
Gas	$_____
Water	$_____
Cell Phone	$_____
Allowance	$_____

Income	
_____.	$_____
_____.	$_____
_____.	$_____
Total: $_____	

Savings	
Starting Balance	$_____
Deposit	$_____
Deposit	$_____
Deposit	$_____
Ending Balance	$_____

Monthly Budgeted Amount	
Entertainment	$_____
Clothing	$_____
Home	$_____
Eating Out	$_____
Travel	$_____
Medical	$_____
Auto	$_____
Christmas	$_____
	$_____
	$_____
	$_____
Ending Balance $_____	

Monthly Goals	
Projected	**Actual**
2% Increase	
2% Decrease	
Debt Paid Off	
Debts Paid Toward	
Total Amount Paid	

Month 8

MON	TUE	WED	THU	FRI	SAT	SUN

Month at a Glance	
Starting Balance	Month

Bills	
Home	$_____
Auto	$_____
Auto Insurance	$_____
Gasoline	$_____
Groceries	$_____
Electric	$_____
Gas	$_____
Water	$_____
Cell Phone	$_____
Allowance	$_____

Income	
_____.	$_____
_____.	$_____
_____.	$_____
Total: $_____	

Savings	
Starting Balance	$_____
Deposit	$_____
Deposit	$_____
Deposit	$_____
Ending Balance	$_____

Monthly Budgeted Amount	
Entertainment	$_____
Clothing	$_____
Home	$_____
Eating Out	$_____
Travel	$_____
Medical	$_____
Auto	$_____
Christmas	$_____
	$_____
	$_____
	$_____
Ending Balance $_____	

Monthly Goals	
Projected	**Actual**
2% Increase	
2% Decrease	
Debt Paid Off	
Debts Paid Toward	
Total Amount Paid	

Month 9

MON	TUE	WED	THU	FRI	SAT	SUN

Month at a Glance	
Starting Balance	Month

Bills	
Home	$_____
Auto	$_____
Auto Insurance	$_____
Gasoline	$_____
Groceries	$_____
Electric	$_____
Gas	$_____
Water	$_____
Cell Phone	$_____
Allowance	$_____

Income	
_____.	$_____
_____.	$_____
_____.	$_____
Total: $_____	

Savings	
Starting Balance	$_____
Deposit	$_____
Deposit	$_____
Deposit	$_____
Ending Balance	$_____

Monthly Budgeted Amount	
Entertainment	$_____
Clothing	$_____
Home	$_____
Eating Out	$_____
Travel	$_____
Medical	$_____
Auto	$_____
Christmas	$_____
	$_____
	$_____
	$_____
Ending Balance $_____	

Monthly Goals	
Projected	**Actual**
2% Increase	
2% Decrease	
Debt Paid Off	
Debts Paid Toward	
Total Amount Paid	

Month 10

MON	TUE	WED	THU	FRI	SAT	SUN

Month at a Glance	
Starting Balance	Month

Bills	
Home	$_____
Auto	$_____
Auto Insurance	$_____
Gasoline	$_____
Groceries	$_____
Electric	$_____
Gas	$_____
Water	$_____
Cell Phone	$_____
Allowance	$_____

Income	
_____ .	$_____
_____ .	$_____
_____ .	$_____
Total: $_____	

Savings	
Starting Balance	$_____
Deposit	$_____
Deposit	$_____
Deposit	$_____
Ending Balance	$_____

Monthly Budgeted Amount	
Entertainment	$_____
Clothing	$_____
Home	$_____
Eating Out	$_____
Travel	$_____
Medical	$_____
Auto	$_____
Christmas	$_____
	$_____
	$_____
	$_____
Ending Balance $_____	

Monthly Goals	
Projected	**Actual**
2% Increase	
2% Decrease	
Debt Paid Off	
Debts Paid Toward	
Total Amount Paid	

Month 11

MON	TUE	WED	THU	FRI	SAT	SUN

Month at a Glance	
Starting Balance	Month

Bills	
Home	$_____
Auto	$_____
Auto Insurance	$_____
Gasoline	$_____
Groceries	$_____
Electric	$_____
Gas	$_____
Water	$_____
Cell Phone	$_____
Allowance	$_____

Income	
_____.	$_____
_____.	$_____
_____.	$_____
Total: $_____	

Savings	
Starting Balance	$_____
Deposit	$_____
Deposit	$_____
Deposit	$_____
Ending Balance	$_____

Monthly Budgeted Amount	
Entertainment	$_____
Clothing	$_____
Home	$_____
Eating Out	$_____
Travel	$_____
Medical	$_____
Auto	$_____
Christmas	$_____
	$_____
	$_____
	$_____
Ending Balance $_____	

Monthly Goals	
Projected	**Actual**
2% Increase	
2% Decrease	
Debt Paid Off	
Debts Paid Toward	
Total Amount Paid	

Month 12

MON	TUE	WED	THU	FRI	SAT	SUN

Month at a Glance	
Starting Balance	Month

Bills	
Home	$_____
Auto	$_____
Auto Insurance	$_____
Gasoline	$_____
Groceries	$_____
Electric	$_____
Gas	$_____
Water	$_____
Cell Phone	$_____
Allowance	$_____

Income	
_____.	$_____
_____.	$_____
_____.	$_____
Total: $_____	

Savings	
Starting Balance	$_____
Deposit	$_____
Deposit	$_____
Deposit	$_____
Ending Balance	$_____

Monthly Budgeted Amount	
Entertainment	$_____
Clothing	$_____
Home	$_____
Eating Out	$_____
Travel	$_____
Medical	$_____
Auto	$_____
Christmas	$_____
	$_____
	$_____
	$_____
Ending Balance $_____	

Monthly Goals	
Projected	**Actual**
2% Increase	
2% Decrease	
Debt Paid Off	
Debts Paid Toward	
Total Amount Paid	

Part III

THE 2% DECREASE

Brainstorm Your Way to Cutting 2% Again and Again

Instructions: Use this questionnaire when filling our your monthly budget to find those 2% cuts. We encourage you to start with the head-smack expenses as they can help find ways to cut easily those first few months.

1. Find those head-smack expenses.

   Check whether you have any of the following expenses that can be easily cut.

☐	Subscriptions (e.g., service, product, or magazine subscriptions)
☐	Unused/underused memberships
☐	Any services that auto-renew each month or year
☐	Check itemized bills for unnecessary fees (e.g., move to paperless billing to avoid fees, ring tone subscriptions)
☐	Check cell phone and other services to determine if you are overpaying (e.g., not using all the data you're paying for on your cell phone thus able to downgrade)

2. List your favorite tips found in Chapters 11-13 to find your next set of 2% cuts for the next several months:

_____

_____

_____

Normal Shopping and Price Comparison List

Write down the items you normally buy and keep track of the prices at the three stores you shop at most. This list is your reference so when you need to purchase that item you can check this list for the lowest everyday price. Plus if the item goes on sale, you can use this list to determine your price point and whether that sale is better than another store's price. See Chapter 13 for more information.

Store Price Comparison			
Item	Store #1	Store #2	Store #3
_____	_____	_____	_____
_____	_____	_____	_____
_____	_____	_____	_____
_____	_____	_____	_____
_____	_____	_____	_____
_____	_____	_____	_____
_____	_____	_____	_____
_____	_____	_____	_____
_____	_____	_____	_____
_____	_____	_____	_____
_____	_____	_____	_____

The No Food Waste Menu Planner

Refer to thethriftycouple.com/menu for details on how to use this menu planner. This planner is amazing as it helps you identify foods that need to be used which ultimately helps you save a lot of money.

Store Price Comparison						
	Breakfast	**Lunch**	**Dinner (Entree)**		**Dinner (Sides)**	
			Dish	Foods	Dish	Foods
Sunday						
Monday						
Tuesday						
Wednesday						
Thursday						
Friday						
Saterday						
Snacks (Week ideas):_____						

Foods to Use This Week	
Fridge	
Pantry	
Freezer	
Notes	

Shopping List

Christmas Savings Planner

Work through this questionnaire to help you determine the amount you need to save either per paycheck or per month. Don't forget to read in Chapter 11 how to stretch that budget even further.

1. How much do I need to set aside for Christmas?

    Answer the following questions based on your best estimation.

Estimated Expenses	
How much we need for gifts:	
Amount needed for travel:	
Needed for decor:	
Other foreseen expenses:	
Total:	

Estimate Budget Based on 1% Gross Income:	
Total Gross Annual Household Income:	
Christmas Fund Percent	1%
Your Christmas Fund	

2. Based on your estimated expenses will 1% of your income be enough?

   If not, how much extra money will you need this next year? Be sure to read the tips in Chapter 11 to find out how to spread out your allocated 1% Christmas Fund further. If you estimate that you will need more based on your initial estimates above, calculate how much extra you will need to save above that 1%. As explained in the book, if you desire to spend more than 1%, this needs to be outside of your 2% increase/decrease so that you can continue to make process towards your financial goals.

   Extra Amount Needed: _____

3. Adding your 1% plus the extra amount, calculate the per paycheck or monthly amount to be saved:

Total Christmas Fund	_____
Number of months or paychecks	_____
Monthly or paycheck amount	_____

Part IV

THE 2% INCREASE

Brainstorming Your Path Towards Earning Extra Income

Instructions: We ultimately encourage you to find ways to utilize your family's talents and gifts to meet and even exceed that 2% increase each month through side hustles or a family side business. However as you work through this worksheet, consider the amount you need, your time and resources and find the method to earn extra income that fits your family best and you can get started with now. Keep your mind open and don't discount any idea as those crazy "out of the world" ideas might be the one that just might work for your family. See Chapters 10 & 14 for more information.

Check out http://thethriftycouple.com/extra-income for even more ideas.

How much do I need per month for my 2% increase?

Short Term Brainstorming

1. How much time does you and your family have available?

_____

_____

_____

2. Do you have any chunks of time you could set aside for this money-making venture?

_____

_____

_____

3. Have you done a side hustle before? If so do you still have the equipment for it?

_____

_____

_____

4. Does any of your friends have a side hustle you could either help them with or learn from them how to do the same?

_____

_____

_____

5. Can you offer a service of some kind?

_____

_____

_____

6. Are there any opportunities you have seen recently that sound intriguing? That sound like something you could put up with for a short time?

_____

_____

_____

How much do I need per month for my 2% increase?

Short Term Brainstorming

1. How much time does you and your family have available?

_____

_____

_____

2. Do you have any chunks of time you could set aside for this money-making venture?

_____

_____

_____

3. Have you done a side hustle before? If so do you still have the equipment for it?

_____

_____

_____

4. Does any of your friends have a side hustle you could either help them with or learn from them how to do the same?

_____

_____

_____

5. Can you offer a service of some kind?

_____

_____

_____

6. Are there any opportunities you have seen recently that sound intriguing? That sound like something you could put up with for a short time?

_____

_____

_____

Longer Term Brainstorming
Note: Some short term brainstorm ideas can translate into long-term answers as well

1. What hobbies do you have you could transform into a money maker?

_____

_____

_____

2. What are you passionate about? Is there some way you could see yourself making money from this?

_____

_____

_____

3. What talents and skills do you and your family members have?

_____

_____

_____

4. Are you or a member of your family an expert in something?

_____

_____

_____

5. Have you considered on-line work-at-home opportunities?

_____

_____

_____

Based on your answers from the questions above:
What are the top 3 ideas to earn extra income short or long term?

_____

_____

_____

Meet with your family and discuss the ideas you have compiled and how you might proceed in executing on those ideas.

_____

_____

_____

Initial Plan for Your Extra Income Opportunity

After finding the right opportunity for you and your family to use to bring in that extra income, use the following form to help you organize and plan basic requirements needed to get started. Reuse this sheet with each new idea you consider. See Chapter 14 for additional information.

Money Making Idea:

Tasks Assigned to Each Family Member:

_____

_____

_____

Items/Resources Needed:

	Estimated		
	Quantity	Unit Price	Total Price
Item			

Marketing Ideas

What is your primary method to contacting potential customers?

_____

_____

_____

Steps to create an online presence	
☐	Reserve a domain name (if needed)
☐	Setup a WordPress blog or otherwise
☐	Create Facebook business page
☐	Create Twitter account
☐	Create Instagram account
☐	Other?

Can you incentivize current customers to spread the word for you?

_____

_____

_____

Estimated Charge for Products/Services:

Estimated Profits:

Goals

Immediate (1-3 months):	

Short Term (3 months – 1 year):	
Longer Term (1-5 years):	

What type of investment is needed to open the doors?

_____

_____

_____

Is there anything else you need to consider to make this successful?

_____

_____

_____

Part V

Moving Forward

Invest In Your 401(k) Up To The Company Match

Instructions: Work through this sheet to find out whether your company has a 401(k) match, how much, and what you need to do to maximize that match. See Chapter 17 for more information.

1. Does your company offer a 401(k) match?

   If you answer no to this question, then we will be talking about retirement in a later step. This is only intended to keep you from throwing away free money from your employer.

   ☐ Yes   ☐ No

2. Gather some information from your company

2a. What is the maximum match percentage your employer will make?

_____

_____

_____

2b. Confirm whether your company has a vesting schedule. When is your fund fully vested?

_____

_____

_____

2c. Does your company match at a certain a "matching percent"?

_____

_____

_____

3. Calculate the recommended amount you will invest this year:

3a. What is your annual pre-tax income?

3b. Calculate the amount you should contribute to your account:

    Annual Income   X   Maximum Match %   = Amount to fund

3c. Calculate the employer match:

    Annual Income   X   Maximum Match %   X   Matching %   = Employer match

3d. Total funded this year:

    Amount to fund   +   Employer match   =   Total Year Funding of 401(k)

Determine Your 3-6 Month Savings Goal

Use the easy steps below to determine your long-term savings goal for 3-6 months of income. Remember this is always about your family and your expectations—not about someone else's expectations on you. Go through this with your family and find out how long it will take you to reach your total goal. It just might surprise you how quickly you'll be able to reach that! See Chapter 15 for more information.

Total Monthly Expenses:	
3-Month Expenses (Monthly X 3):	
6-Month Expenses (Monthly X 6):	
Our Family's Goal:	
Expected Amount You Can Save Monthly:	
Approximate # of Months (Goal / Monthly Savings):	
Goal Date for Reaching 3-6 Months of Savings:	

Determine Your Own Percentage Based Finances

Using the questions and information in Chapter 16 to determine the appropriate percentage of your income that will be allotted to these categories every time you get paid. Remember this sheet is intended to be filled out only after you are consumer debt free so don't become frustrated if you're not there yet. This plan will keep your finances in check and help prevent you from going back into debt again.

Total Monthly Net Income:		
Category	% to set aside	Amount per Month (% X Monthly Net)
Charity		
Christmas		
Vacation		
Home Improvement		
Car		
College/Education		
Retirement		
Totals:		

Mortgage Payoff Checklist

Work through this questionnaire to take those baby steps towards a paid-off mortgage! Reference Chapter 18 for additional information to help you through this process.

Baseline: *From your current amortization schedule (use an online mortgage calculator if needed) record your monthly payments with expected payoff if you didn't change your current payoff strategy.*

Mortgage Balance:	
Interest Rate:	
Payoff Date:	

Step #1: Implement a Bi-Weekly Payment System: *Determine your bi-weekly payment amount by dividing your current payment in half. Use an online mortgage calculator to find the amount of interest saved and determine your new payoff date for your loan.*

Bi-weekly amount:	
Goal Start Date:	
Actual Start Date:	
Interest Saved:	
New Payoff Date:	

Step #2: Round up your bi-weekly payments to the nearest $100 amount: *Increase your bi-weekly payment amount up to the next $100. Use an online mortgage calculator to find the amount of interest saved and determine your new payoff date for your loan.*

New Bi-weekly amount:	
Implementation Date:	
Interest Saved:	
New Payoff Date:	

Step #3: Pay as much extra as you can, when you can: *No matter the amount, those extra payments will add up over time. Use the following, however, to track any additional amounts applied to your mortgage over $500 to see your new-found goal in sight with the addition of those individual large payments.*

Date	Amount	Extra Interest Saved	New Payoff Date

Step #4: Implement 7-10 Plan Gradually: *Each time you increase your bi-weekly amount you are getting closer to your goal of paying off your mortgage in 7-10 years (or less!). Keep finding ways you can increase your bi-weekly payments.*

Original Bi-weekly Payment:	(see Step #1)	
Goal Bi-weekly payment:		

Date	New Bi-Weekly Payment	Left to Goal (Goal – New Payment)

Step #5: 7-10 Mortgage Plan Reached: *This is a huge accomplishment and you are now well on your way to paying off your mortgage. Record the "worst case" scenario payoff date.*

Date Accomplished:	
New Payoff Date:	

Brainstorm Ideas to Pay Off Mortgage Even Earlier:

Find and Fund your Roth IRA

Work through this worksheet to determine important considerations how to open your Roth IRA. See Chapter 17 for more information.

Considerations before you contribute to a Roth IRA this year

Note: Current rules change each year. Check a site like rothira.com for more information.

1. What is your filing status?

_____

_____

_____

2. What is your annual income (specifically your Modified Adjusted Gross Income)?

_____

_____

_____

3. Are you over 50? Previous years have allowed additional contributions.

_____

_____

_____

4. Check the rules for the current year with your filing status and annual income make you eligible to contribute to a Roth IRA.

_____

_____

_____

5. How much can you contribute to a Roth IRA this year? If married, then both of you can contribute to separate accounts.

_____

_____

_____

6. Don't forget you can open and contribute to a "current year" Roth IRA through the tax deadline (generally April 15) of the following year.

_____

_____

_____

Determine what is important to you when looking for a company to manage your Roth IRA

☐ No minimum balance

☐ No/low per trade commissions

☐ Promotion for opening a Roth IRA with their company

☐ Access to a human advisor

☐ More automated control of your portfolio (less hands on)

☐ A low management fee for hand-off investing

☐ More control of your investments?

☐ 24/7 customer support

☐ Higher percentage of your portfolio in active trading

☐ Higher percentage of your portfolio in mutual funds

Made in the USA
San Bernardino, CA
11 November 2017